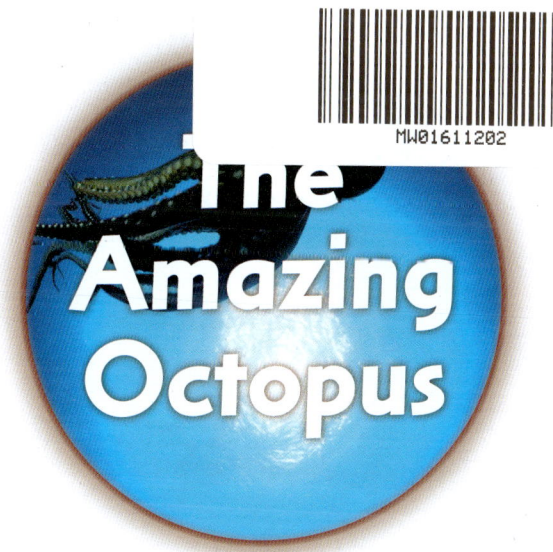

The Amazing Octopus

by Cindy Baker

HOUGHTON MIFFLIN HARCOURT
School Publishers

ILLUSTRATION CREDIT: 5 © Diane Blasius

PHOTOGRAPHY CREDITS: Cover © Juniors Bildarchiv/Alamy; 1 © Corbis/SuperStock; 2 © Juniors Bildarchiv/Alamy; 3 © Corbis/SuperStock; 4 © Digital Vision/Alamy; 6 © Jeffrey L. Rotman/Corbis; 7 © Chris Newbert; 8 © Ralph A. Clevenger/Corbis; 9 © Fred Bavendam; 10 © Herve Lavigne/Alamy

Printed in China

ISBN-13: 978-0-547-02709-8
ISBN-10: 0-547-02709-5

3 4 5 6 7 8 0940 18 17 16 15 14 13 12 11 10

suction cups

What amazing animal has eight arms but no hands? The answer is an octopus!

The octopus uses its arms to crawl along on the ocean floor. Each arm has 240 suction cups. They help the octopus move through the water.

How an Octopus Moves

Sometimes the octopus needs to move fast. The octopus fills its body with water. Then it pushes the water out. The octopus speeds through the water. It can go as fast as 25 miles an hour!

What an Octopus Eats

Octopuses eat many animals. They eat crabs and fish. Large octopuses can eat sharks!

Octopuses use their arms to look for food. The little cups on their arms can grip the food that they find.

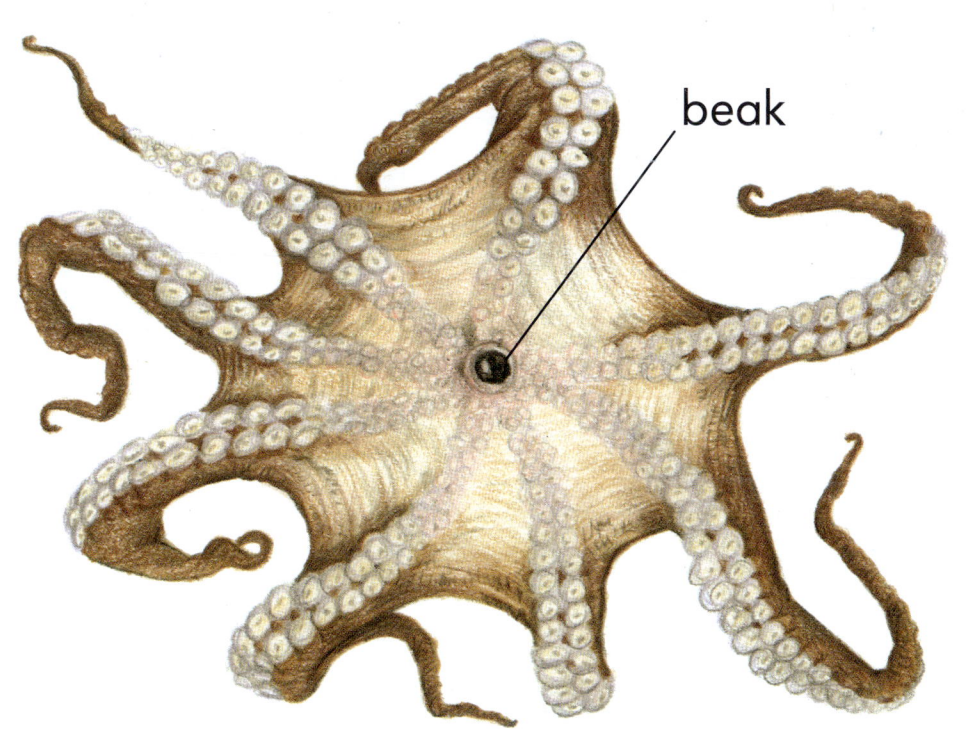

beak

An octopus also looks in places where animals hide. It looks for food in small, dark places. Its arms reach far into the rocks.

The octopus has a beak in its mouth. The beak breaks open the shells of lobsters and clams.

Octopus Size

Octopuses are many different sizes. One of the biggest octopuses has arms that are six feet long.

Baby octopuses are quite small. A really tiny baby is no bigger than a freckle.

Octopus Colors

Octopuses can change colors. This helps them hide from danger. Octopuses show their feelings, too. They change colors when they are mad or happy!

Octopuses are also very smart. They are smart enough to open jars!

Octopus Bodies

Octopuses don't have shells. Their bodies are soft. This makes it easy for octopuses to hide. They can squeeze into tiny places.

Sometimes an octopus gets hurt and loses an arm. The arm grows right back!

ink

Octopus Ink

If an enemy attacks an octopus, the octopus can squirt ink in the water. This ink is not like the ink you find in a blue or black pen. The ink hurts the enemy's eyes, so the octopus can swim away quickly.

Octopuses live all over the world. They swim in cold water and warm water. Some people think they look scary, but they don't want to hurt you. Octopuses are amazing animals!

Responding

✓ TARGET SKILL **Author's Purpose**

Why did the author write this book? What are three details that help tell you this? Make a chart.

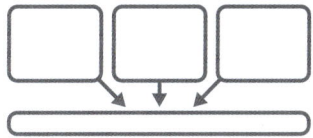

✏ Write About It

Text to World Draw a picture of an octopus. Write two sentences that tell facts about octopuses.

WORDS TO KNOW

blue	little	water
cold	live	where
far	their	

LEARN MORE WORDS

crawl	suction

TARGET SKILL **Author's Purpose**

Tell why an author writes a book.

TARGET STRATEGY **Analyze/Evaluate**

Tell how you feel about the text, and why.

GENRE **Informational text** gives facts about a topic.